WHAT WOULD YOU CHOOSE?

MEGA
MACHINES

HELEN GREATHEAD

EDGE
FRANKLIN WATTS

LONDON·SYDNEY

Franklin Watts

First published in Great Britain in 2015
by The Watts Publishing Group

Series editor: Adrian Cole

Art direction: Peter Scoulding

Series designer: D. R. ink

Picture researcher: Diana Morris

Dewey number 621.8
HB ISBN 978 1 4451 4215 9
Library ebook ISBN 978 1 4451 4217 3

Printed in China

Franklin Watts

An imprint of
Hachette Children's Group
Part of The Watts Publishing Group
Carmelite House
50 Victoria Embankment
London EC4Y 0DZ

An Hachette UK Company
www.hachette.co.uk
www.franklinwatts.co.uk

MIX
Paper from
responsible sources
FSC® C104740

FSC
www.fsc.org

CONTENTS

WOULD YOU CHOOSE

TO SEE THE WORLD ON A PENNY-FARTHING, GO TO SCHOOL RIDING A HOVERBOARD OR TAKE OFF FOR PARIS IN A FLYING CAR?

Mega Machines invites you to belt up, discover all manner of amazing machines and decide which ones you'd rather try out.

Read each question, CONSIDER YOUR OPTIONS, check out the facts,

see what your friends think (and what we chose) and then make YOUR choice.

RIDE WITH THE COPS IN ITALY ... OR UKRAINE?

WE CHOSE

Italy. In 2003, cash-strapped Ukrainian police used a metal cut-out cop car to fool speeding drivers into slowing down. In Italy in 2014, Lamborghini donated one of their Huracán supercars (below) to the Italian police force. It can zoom from 0 to 60 in just 3.2 seconds and hit a top speed of 325 kph! It features all-wheel-drive, is fitted with a number-plate recognition camera and can flash instant images back to police headquarters.

Didn't you know?
Dubai's police force has a whole fleet of supercars, including a MacLaren MP4-12C, an Aston Martin 177, a Lamborghini Aventador and a Ferrari FF.

SECURE YOUR BIKE WITH A SOLAR-POWERED LOCK ... OR RIDE ALONG A SOLAR BIKE TRACK?

WE CHOSE

The lock. Solar cells in each 100 metres of Dutch bike track soak up rays that provide enough electricity to power three homes, but they won't help your bike. The bike lock, however, is intelligent! The Skylock runs on a solar-powered, rechargeable battery. Used with a smartphone, it will unlock at a distance and let you know if anyone's tampering with your bike. Should you have an accident, the lock will automatically message your family.

THE FACTS

THE PENNY-FARTHING
- was invented in 1871 and got its name because the wheel sizes reminded people of the size difference between a penny coin and a farthing coin around at the time
- has one fixed gear and a hard leather saddle
- has solid rubber tyres and a cast iron frame
- has a 1.5 m front wheel that was designed for increased speed and a smoother ride

SEE THE WORLD ON A PENNY-FARTHING ... OR A GO-KART?

THE FACTS

THE GO-KART
- was first raced in a Californian car park in the 1950s
- became a massive craze in the 1960s
- hasn't changed much since the 1970s, though there are many different makes and sizes
- can reach speeds of up to 100 kph
- is powered by 2- and 4-stroke engines, or electric motors

WHAT'S SO SPECIAL ABOUT THE PENNY-FARTHING?

The penny-farthing made cycling history with its high-quality ride and superior speed.

BUT YOU WOULDN'T GO ROUND THE WORLD ON ONE?

Thomas Stevens did, from 1884 to 1887. He travelled 21,762 km carrying a pistol and his raincoat, which doubled as a tent. Then, in 2008, Joff Summerfield (above) did it too. He visited four continents, 23 countries and covered 35,406 km, and even crossed the Himalayas and reached Everest base camp!

WHAT'S SO SPECIAL ABOUT KARTING?

Karting isn't just for kids, it's the cheapest form of four-wheeled motor sport there is. Some of the earliest go-karts used lawn-mower engines and were sold in kits. Today some Superkarts, with up to 500 cc engines, race at over 225 kph!

BUT YOU WOULDN'T TAKE ONE AROUND THE WORLD?

Stan Mott did from 1961 to 1964. His kart (and trailer) stood 5 cm off the ground (below). He fitted headlights and a 175cc Lambretta engine. He covered 61,155 km and visited 29 countries. He even drove his go-kart across the Sahara Desert!

AND FINALLY...

You can fall off the penny-farthing, you can't carry many supplies and it's slow going — 64 km a day on average! You probably won't fall out of the go-kart, but you'll be hard to spot in traffic, you'll have to pay for fuel, and there are lots of parts that might need fixing.

WE CHOSE

Get on the bike. You're less likely to break down, and you'll get a better view!

ARRIVE AT THE SCHOOL PROM IN A MINI COOPER ... OR A ROLLS-ROYCE PHANTOM?

WE CHOSE

The Mini. The Phantom may look beautiful and have a luxurious interior, but we're talking an 8.2-metre stretch Mini Cooper that can seat six of you in comfort. You can even get the party started on its dance-floor that comes complete with flashing lights, and a surround-sound music system!

TRAVEL HOME BY OUTDOOR ESCALATOR ... OR UNDERGROUND FUNICULAR?

WE CHOSE

The escalator. It takes 8 minutes to travel 1.8 km to the top of Israel's Carmelit Funicular, in Haifa, without a view (top left). The escalator in Medellín, Colombia (bottom left), is 3.85 km long, as tall as a 28-storey building and you can travel to the top in just 6 minutes. Medellín was once the world's murder capital, but the escalator has helped to reduce crime by providing poorer people with an easy way to reach the city centre.

RACE A MONSTER TRUCK ... OR A SNOWMOBILE?

Didn't you know?
In 2014, the Raminator broke the world speed record for monster trucks – at 159.48 kph. It took years of careful engineering to create the Raminator, which stands 3 m tall and 3.8 m wide.

A monster truck has a lightweight fibreglass body which looks like an ordinary truck or car, combined with the most enormous tyres and a massive engine. Most monster trucks are capable of up to 110 kph, but won't go that fast during a circuit race when you leap over ramps and crush cars.

On a snowmobile you're low to the ground, holding handlebars that direct the skis at the front, while a rotating track grips the ice at the back. Snowmobile riders in the Winter X-Games perform amazing stunts during the snowmobile freestyle event. They speed up ice ramps and can even do mid-air flips!

AND FINALLY...

Both vehicles are dangerous – monster trucks have even killed spectators on more than one occasion, but there are hundreds of snowmobile accidents a year in the USA alone.

WE CHOSE

The monster truck. It may not be as fast, but you stand more chance of getting to the end of the race.

THE FACTS

THE EXOSKELETON:
- can change positions from standing to lying virtually flat for maximum speed
- can reach a top speed of 120 kph
- runs on high-energy-density batteries with zero carbon emissions
- is lightweight, but stable thanks to its sturdy backbone

RIDE A THREE-WHEELED EXOSKELETON ... OR IN A THREE-WHEEL CAR?

THE FACTS

THE i-ROAD:
- has one wheel at the back and two 2 kilowatt electric motors
- can cover up to 48 km on one charge
- has a top speed of 48 kph
- is only 850 mm wide, but seats two people (front and back)

Didn't you know?
The i-Road is so small that four of them will fit in one normal-sized parking space!

TELL ME ABOUT THE EXOSKELETON

It was designed by Pasadena Arts Centre Student, Jake Loniak, as a completely different way of travelling. Thirty-six pneumatic muscles control the legs, arms and backbone of the vehicle and protect the rider.

WHAT'S IT LIKE TO RIDE?

Actually, you don't ride this machine so much as *wear* it – even the helmet is built in! The frame supports your body, but your body controls the machine. You'll shift positions depending on where you're driving, but at top speed you'll feel like you're flying just above the road surface.

TELL ME ABOUT THE i-ROAD

It's designed to look like a motorbike, but with the comfort and protection of a car (so no helmet needed). The three wheels make it more stable than a bike, but it's only designed for short journeys, so it won't go far before it needs a recharge.

WHAT'S THE i-ROAD LIKE TO DRIVE?

Inside feels more like a cockpit than a normal car; the controls are simple to use and once you're rolling it even feels like you're gliding. The i-Road is easy to manoeuvre, with the back wheel swivelling to steer. It's even designed so you can't tip it over.

AND FINALLY...

The Exoskeleton hasn't actually been built yet; it needs to pass a lot of tests before it can be used on the road. The i-Road is tried, tested and due to launch in 2015.

WE CHOSE

The I-Road. It's so like a motorbike it even leans into corners!

WHAT WOULD YOU CHOOSE?

RIDE THE WORLD'S STEEPEST STEEL ROLLERCOASTER ... OR THE WORLD'S FASTEST?

WE CHOSE

The fastest. The steepest rollercoaster has views of Mount Fuji, Japan. You will free-fall a stomach-flipping 43 m at 121 degrees, reaching speeds of up to 100 kph (below). However, the fastest rollercoaster at Ferrari World, in Dubai (left), travels at a top speed of 240 kph! You'll need safety goggles as you swish round the tracks in a Formula One Ferrari-style car.

KEEP A FLYING PIGEON ... OR A WASP IN YOUR HOME?

WE CHOSE

The Vespa (it's Italian for wasp) because it's got more vroom! With just one gear and a sturdy black frame, the Flying Pigeon is the most popular bicycle EVER. Owning one in China in the 1950s was a sign of prosperity. The Vespa motor scooter was first produced in Italy in 1946. With its neat design, which protected the engine and its rider, Vespas were soon popular all over the world.

Didn't you know?
Over 75 million Flying Pigeons have been produced since 1950.

GO TO SCHOOL ON A MOTORISED SKATEBOARD ... OR A HOVERBOARD?

The idea for the Hoverboard – a floating skateboard – came from the 1989 movie *Back to the Future: Part II*. In 2014 'hovering' was finally made possible through electromagnetic technology. The 'Hendo' hoverboard can carry two people, floating 3 cm above the ground, for around 15 minutes.

The motorised skateboard has two motors hidden under the board to turn the back wheels. A handheld control lets you move forward, slow down and stop. You can't do tricks on these boards, but you'll coast uphill and ride for up to 10 km at a maximum speed of 32 kph.

AND FINALLY...

Even if your journey to school takes under 15 minutes, it's unlikely you'd get there on a Hoverboard. Because of its electromagnetic technology, it only works on certain metal surfaces. The skateboard doesn't come cheap, but it should get you to school no trouble.

WE CHOSE

The skateboard. If the battery runs out, you can always move it with your foot!

REMOTE-CONTROLLED TANK ... OR DRIVERLESS TRUCK?

THE FACTS

THE TANK BULLDOZER, OR TERRIER:

- weighs 29 tonnes, is 6 m long and 2.5 m wide
- has a top speed of 72 kph
- uses five onboard cameras to get 360 degree views night and day, whatever the conditions
- can be operated by what looks like a games console over half a kilometre away!

WHAT ELSE CAN THE TERRIER DO?

With its various attachments, the Terrier can dig holes, drill concrete, lift objects, clear minefields and, thanks to its caterpillar tracks, cross ditches up to 2 m wide. When operators are inside its cab they can defend themselves with the Terrier's machine gun and smoke grenades.

WHAT'S THE POINT OF THE TERRIER?

The tank gives protection to the troops who use it. Its remote control means, in certain dangerous situations, its operators can keep a safe distance.

Didn't you know?
The Terrier can move up to 270 tonnes of earth in an hour – that's about the volume of two double-decker buses!

THE FACTS

THE MERCEDES FUTURE TRUCK 2025:

- drives itself automatically, and knows when a vehicle is overtaking because of its outside motion sensors
- is powered by a 12.8 litre, 6 cylinder diesel engine
- can see up to 100 m ahead, thanks to a 3-D camera that detects cars, pedestrians, objects in the road, road markings and traffic signs
- can connect to the Internet to communicate with other vehicles

WHAT ELSE CAN THE TRUCK DO?

The Future Truck can maintain a steady speed on boring motorway journeys, keeping fuel consumption low, and freeing drivers to do other work. They have to stay awake though, or the truck will slow down and pull over.

WHAT'S THE POINT OF BEING DRIVERLESS?

Around the world, an average of 3,400 people die on the roads each day. Most accidents are caused by human error. Computers don't get tired, so the driverless truck won't lose concentration.

Didn't you know?
The inspiration for the look of the Future Truck came from outfits worn by French pop band, Daft Punk.

AND FINALLY...

While 60 Terriers are already at work with the British Army, the Future Truck is just that – a truck of the future. The technology is available though, and could make 24-hour deliveries more efficient. However, laws need to change before we will see driverless vehicles on the roads.

WE CHOSE

The Terrier – but grab that console and stand well back!

TRAVEL FROM LONDON TO PARIS BY EUROSTAR TRAIN ... OR FLYING CAR?

Eighteen Eurostar trains travel between London and Paris each day, covering the 343.9 km in 2 hours 15 minutes. The larger trains are just under half a kilometre long, and can carry up to 770 passengers. Just over 50 km of the journey is via the Channel Tunnel, 50–75 m below the sea!

Drive your Aeromobil to the nearest airfield, press a button to open out the wings, adjust the gears to power the propeller and switch to flying controls. With a top speed of 200 kph and a distance of 692 km, the Aeromobil could make it to Paris in under two hours, using far less fuel than a car when it's gliding.

Didn't you know?
The Aeromobil is small enough to slot into a single parking space.

AND FINALLY...

You can land the Aeromobil in a farmer's field, but it will need a clear 50 m, and 200 m for takeoff – that's hard to find in the city centre. Step straight from the Eurostar in London or Paris, and you're quickly connected with public transport.

WE CHOSE

Eurostar. Glide into the city on a set of rails.

3-D PRINT YOUR OWN HOUSE ... OR CAR?

Building began on the world's first 3-D printed house in Amsterdam at the beginning of 2014. It needed a specially built 3-D printer that's 6 m tall to make plastic parts that will become the walls of this futuristic structure. The plan is to recycle plastic waste to make new homes in overcrowded cities around the world.

WE CHOSE

The car – for now. While the house is just a prototype, which will hopefully be used around the world one day, the car actually works.

The first ever 3-D printed car was also designed and made in 2014 from 49 printed body parts – instead of the usual 5,000! The tyres, wheels, electric battery, suspension and windscreen were made in the usual way, but the body, chassis and dashboard were printed from black plastic, reinforced with carbon fibre. It all took just 44 hours.

RIDE A TRAIN THAT FLOATS ABOVE THE TRACKS ... OR A BOAT THAT FLOATS OVER WATER?

THE FACTS

THE MAGLEV TRAIN:
- doesn't have wheels
- doesn't have an engine, so it doesn't give off harmful emissions
- doesn't really have a proper driver

THE FACTS

A HOVERCRAFT:
- floats on a cushion of air
- is amphibious: it can come out of the water to land on any flattish surface
- uses half as much fuel as a same-sized boat and can travel twice as fast

HOW DOES A MAGLEV MOVE?

Maglev is short for magnetic levitation. Using electromagnetic pull, these trains can float above their tracks, or guideways. Waves of magnetic energy produced by generators in the guideways move the train along.

WHERE CAN I RIDE A MAGLEV?

Shanghai's maglev trains are the fastest passenger trains in the world, running 30 km from the city centre to the airport, with a top speed of 431 kph. Japan's new maglevs won't operate until 2027, but they're expected to make the 322-km journey between Tokyo and Nagoya in just 40 minutes!

SO HOW DOES A HOVERCRAFT MOVE?

A fan forces air into the inflatable rubber cushion underneath the craft and it rises up. The engine creates thrust, to make the craft move forward and the 'pilot' steers the rudder to change direction. The craft floats on air rather than water, so there's no friction between the boat and the water. That's why it can move so fast.

WHERE CAN I RIDE A HOVERCRAFT?

Hovercraft are best used in hard-to-reach areas, such as shallow or icy waters, or mudflats. They're popular with the military, but some people race smaller hovercraft for fun!

Didn't you know?
Experiments with a hair dryer, one tin inside another and some weighing scales helped the hovercraft inventor develop his idea in the 1950s.

AND FINALLY...

Travelling at 100 kph in a hovercraft can be a bumpy experience, but on a maglev train, even at 400 kph, you won't feel the speed.

WE CHOSE

The maglev. One day maglev technology might even be used to launch vehicles into space, reducing the huge cost of fuel used on take off.

LOOK COOL IN A CLASSIC VW BEETLE …
OR A FIAT 500?

The first Volkswagen Beetle was designed by Ferdinand Porsche in 1937 especially for families (bottom left). It was a four-seater, with an air-cooled engine (at the back!), that was cheap to run. The original Beetle proved to be very reliable, and carried on selling until 2003!

The first Fiat 500 was designed by Dante Giacosa in 1957 as Italy's family car (bottom right). Like the Beetle, its air-cooled engine was at the back – the doors opened backwards too. At only 3 m long, it was designed to be affordable – the stylish sun-roof that stretched the length of the roof was actually a way to use less steel!

AND FINALLY...

The Beetle was designed on the orders of Adolf Hitler – definitely not cool! At its launch in 1957, a parade of 500s drove through the streets of Turin, each with a fashion model standing in the back, to a reception from a future Pope, the King of Belgium and other Italian celebrities. Now that was super-cool!

WE CHOSE

The Fiat 500.

Didn't you know?
The Beetle was so well finished it was practically watertight and could float for a few minutes on water!

L·74448

AN E-BIKE ... OR SEGWAY TO RIDE INTO TOWN?

An e-bike looks like an ordinary bike, with an added motor and rechargeable battery. A sensor tells the motor how much help you need with pedalling and, once power assisted, you'll fly uphill! The e-bike's electric engine can't drive the bike faster than 24 kph – but you can!

On a Segway you stand between two wheels, and simply lean forward to speed up, backwards to slow down (there are no brakes!) and left or right to steer. The Segway does your balancing for you, using gyroscopes and a built-in computer, and has a top speed of around 20 kph.

Didn't you know?
You don't 'ride' on a Segway, you 'glide'.

WE CHOSE

The e-bike. In some countries, you can only use a Segway on private roads. However, the European Union has now officially agreed that e-bikes are a healthy, emission-free answer to city-centre traffic trouble.

WHAT WOULD YOU CHOOSE?

This GENeco Bio-Bus is powered by your waste for a sustainable future GENeco

Tell us what you think #biobus

TAKE A BUS FUELLED BY POO ...
OR A SOLAR CAR CALLED STELLA?

THE FACTS

THE BIO-BUS:
- first hit the road in Bath, Somerset, UK, in 2014
- is powered by a renewable and sustainable fuel (human poo and food waste), producing fewer emissions than diesel
- can carry up to 40 people and travel up to 300 km without needing to refuel

Didn't you know?
The side of the bio-bus is decorated with pictures of people sitting on the loo!

HOW MUCH POO DOES THE BUS NEED?

It takes a year's supply of poo from five people to fill the tank just once! The supply isn't likely to run out, however, because Bristol sewage works processes 75 million cubic metres of sewage waste and 35,500 tons of food waste each year!

DOESN'T THE BUS SMELL?

No. Bacteria in the anaerobic digester break down all biodegradable material in the waste to produce biomethane gas, which powers the bus. The impurities are extracted, so the fuel hardly smells at all.

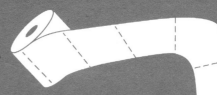

WHAT MAKES STELLA SO GREAT?

Solar panels convert the Sun's rays into electricity and charge Stella's lithium battery. Stella is the first 'energy positive' car (she creates more energy than she uses). The excess energy can charge up other gadgets. She's built from aluminium and carbon fibre and weighs just 380 kg.

HOW FAR CAN SHE GO?

Stella can travel up to 885 km when fully charged, and drive in daylight further than any of today's electric cars. In 2013, Stella won the Cruiser Class in the World Solar Challenge, racing 3,000 km from Darwin to Adelaide, Australia, against other solar cars. She averaged 60 kph, with a top speed of 120 kph.

THE FACTS

STELLA, THE SOLAR-POWERED CAR:
- was developed by a team of Dutch technology students
- is fuelled by solar panels on her roof
- can comfortably carry a family of four with their luggage and travel up to 885 km on one charge
- is 4.6 m long, but only 1.2 m tall

AND FINALLY...

Stella is licensed to go on the road, but she's the only one of her kind so far. Bio-buses don't just exist in Bristol, they're used in other parts of the UK and Sweden too.

WE CHOSE

Public transport wins at the moment, so take the poo-bus, but keep your eyes peeled for more solar-powered cars.

RACE THE PORSCHE P2 SEMPER VIVUS HYBRID ... OR THE FERRARI 125S?

WE CHOSE

The Ferrari – it's the first in a long line of dream cars. Produced in 1900, the P2 (above, left) was the second car made by Porsche and the first hybrid car EVER. The P2 reached 32 kph, and could cover 60 km when fully charged. The first Ferrari EVER, the 125S, was produced 47 years later (above, right). It was designed for speed, and could hit 170 kph and go from 0 to 100 in 10.8 seconds.

TRACK YOUR FITNESS WITH YOUR SMART WATCH ... OR YOUR SMART SHIRT?

WE CHOSE

The shirt. Covering a greater surface area, the smart shirt can keep a larger number of micro-sensors close to your skin, measuring your speed, location and heart rate. It sends the information via a transmitter to a smartphone. Some fabrics can even be recharged when they're washed and ironed!

9.78 km

01:14:22

♥ 142

Pace 7.93 km/h

Calories 534

Didn't you know?
Your shoes can tell you where to go! Connect a pair of 'Haptic' shoes to a smartphone, and they'll vibrate to tell you whether to turn left or right.

TAKE A TOUR ON A HIPPO BUS THAT FLOATS ...
OR A CAMEL BUS WITH HUMPS?

Havana Cuba's camel bus (above) has one cab, two humps and eighteen wheels. Old buses welded unevenly together create the hump effect, while a tractor cab pulls the bus along – with up to 300 commuting passengers inside!

Take a Hippo bus-boat tour in Victoria, Canada (below), and your bus will leave the road and plunge – like a hippo – into the Pacific Ocean! This converted school bus follows the style of military amphibious landing craft, rolling along roads and floating in water.

WE CHOSE

The Hippo. With no air conditioning, Cubans were relieved when the camel buses started going out of service. The Hippo buses are carefully tested, so that their 40 passengers are safe on board to have fun and stay dry (the bus is completely waterproof).

HENRIETTA HIPPO
www.Toronto Hippo Tours.com
416-703-HIPO (4476)
Ride The Hippos
The hippest way to see Toronto

THE FACTS

THE SR-71 'BLACKBIRD':
- is nearly 17 m high and over 32 m long
- can reach speeds over Mach 3.2 at an altitude of 21–26,000 m
- flies at a maximum altitude of 137,000 m

BREAK THE SOUND BARRIER IN A LAND ROCKET ... OR A PLANE THAT FLIES LIKE A ROCKET?

WHAT'S IT LIKE TO FLY A BLACKBIRD?

More like a spaceship than an aircraft, you'll need to wear a pressure suit to survive the altitude. The engine accelerates so fast, that within two minutes of lift-off you're at 7,315 m!

WHAT'S SPECIAL ABOUT THE WAY THE PLANE IS MADE?

After breaking the sound barrier, the temperature soars to over 340 degrees Celsius, but the plane's lightweight titanium body is built to cope with the heat. The Blackbird gets its name from its special black paint that can absorb radar signals. To radar equipment on the ground the plane looks smaller than a person!

WHAT'S IT LIKE TO DRIVE A ROCKET CAR?

At first you'll feel like you're in a plane speeding up for take off, but you'll just keep rolling. Up to 480 kph can feel quite bumpy, then approaching the speed of sound (1236 kph/Mach 1), a shockwave is created and your clear view becomes misty. The noise is incredible!

WHAT'S SPECIAL ABOUT THE BLOODHOUND?

The cockpit is made from a single piece of carbon fibre and took 10,000 hours to design and build. The roof is shaped to slow airflow to the engines at the back. The solid aluminium wheels have to stay on the ground.

THE FACTS

THE BLOODHOUND SSC:
- is around 14 m long and weighs 7.5 tonnes
- is called a supersonic car (SSC), because it's designed to travel faster than the speed of sound
- looks like a rocket, but is classed as a car because it has four wheels and is controlled by a driver

AND FINALLY...

Andy Green's 1997 land speed record of 1,228 kph still stands. No one else has ever broken the sound barrier on land. The Blackbird has flown at over three times the speed of sound (3,500 kph – Mach 3.2) over 1,000 times.

WE CHOSE

The Blackbird. It's not in service any more, but it's still the fastest manned jet plane in the world.

Didn't you know?
The Bloodhound SSC is powered by a jet engine and Formula One engines. They produce 135,000 horsepower – the equivalent of 180 Formula One cars!

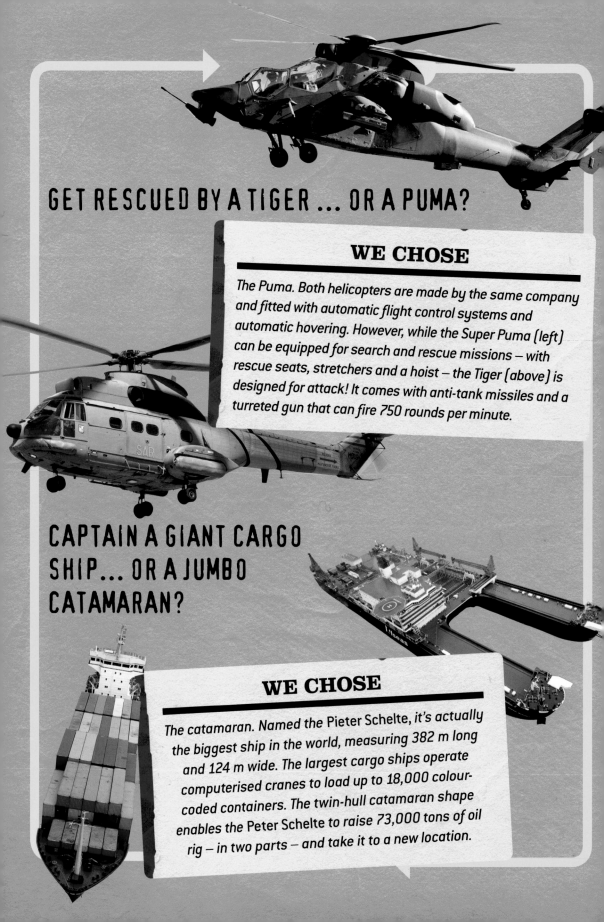

GET RESCUED BY A TIGER ... OR A PUMA?

WE CHOSE

The Puma. Both helicopters are made by the same company and fitted with automatic flight control systems and automatic hovering. However, while the Super Puma (left) can be equipped for search and rescue missions — with rescue seats, stretchers and a hoist — the Tiger (above) is designed for attack! It comes with anti-tank missiles and a turreted gun that can fire 750 rounds per minute.

CAPTAIN A GIANT CARGO SHIP... OR A JUMBO CATAMARAN?

WE CHOSE

The catamaran. Named the Pieter Schelte, it's actually the biggest ship in the world, measuring 382 m long and 124 m wide. The largest cargo ships operate computerised cranes to load up to 18,000 colour-coded containers. The twin-hull catamaran shape enables the Peter Schelte to raise 73,000 tons of oil rig — in two parts — and take it to a new location.

WHAT WOULD YOU CHOOSE?

OBSERVE EARTH FROM ONE HUGE SATELLITE ... OR FROM LOTS OF LITTLE ONES THE SIZE OF A BIRD?

Landsats (below, right) are designed and built by NASA. They've been orbiting and scanning Earth since the 1970s, relaying images showing Earth's changing land and resource use. Large satellites like these can be the size of a small house, weigh over 3,000 kg and take up to ten years to build!

A mini satellite, called the 'Dove' (above), was designed in a garage. It's the size of a shoebox, weighs 5 kg, and has a telescope. Creators of the Dove plan to have 100 of them orbiting Earth at once, to keep track of changes in forestry, fishing, agriculture and climate.

AND FINALLY...

The Landsat costs millions of pounds to build, while the Dove is cheap to make. Landsat 8 scans the whole Earth every 16 days, but the Dove will do this every day.

WE CHOSE

The Dove. Why have one satellite when you can have 100?

Didn't you know?
Disused satellites make up some of the 13,000 items of human-made space junk orbiting our planet that will eventually fall back to Earth.

GO TO THE SEASIDE IN A 1970S VW CAMPER WITH A POP-TOP ROOF ... OR AN ELEMMENT PALAZZO MOTORHOME WITH A POP-UP ROOF TERRACE?

WE CHOSE

The VW Camper. The 12-m-long Elemment Palazzo may have a fridge, dishwasher, and an upstairs with a bedroom, bathroom and roof terrace (which pops up at the push of a button) but it comes with a £2 million price tag. Simply push up the VW Camper pop-top roof by hand and – ta-da – you'll find two bunk beds! Who needs a roof terrace?

MEET A ROBOT THAT CAN READ YOUR EMOTIONS ... OR ONE THAT SHOWS EMOTION?

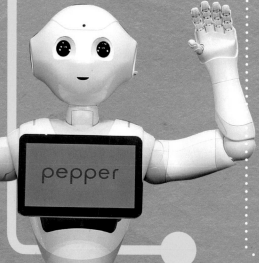

WE CHOSE

The emotion-reading robot called Pepper. The Japanese karakuri robot operates through a clockwork mechanism and shows emotion after he shoots his arrow and it misses. His face seems disappointed! This is 200-year-old technology, though, and the emotion is only a clever illusion. Pepper, however, is a cutting-edge Japanese robot which uses artificial intelligence to read your emotions when he talks to you.

WHAT WOULD
YOU CHOOSE?

GLOSSARY

2-stroke engine – An engine that completes a power cycle with two strokes (two up and down movements) of the piston, rather than four (which happens in a 4-stroke engine).

altitude – Height above the surface of the Earth.

anaerobic digester – A large container where tiny organisms breakdown organic matter (without oxygen).

artificial intelligence – A computer system developed to perform tasks normally requiring human intelligence, such as decision-making.

carbon emissions – Carbon dioxide that is released by vehicles such as cars, planes and buses when they are fuelled by petrol or diesel.

electromagnetic – The use of magnetic fields (of attraction and repulsion) to suspend one object above an another.

exoskeleton – The name for the external skeleton around an insect that supports and protects its body. A powered exoskeleton is worn by a person and boosts their strength or endurance.

friction – Resistance generated when one surface rubs against another.

gear – A metal wheel with 'teeth' that works with other toothed wheels to change the speed of a vehicle or engine.

gyroscope – A device consisting of a wheel or a disc mounted so that it can spin freely about an axis.

hybrid – Refers to a vehicle powered by an electric motor and a conventional engine.

Mach – An unusually high speed – the ratio of the speed of an object compared to the speed of sound.

pneumatic – Containing air or using air pressure to make something move or work.

public transport – Trains, buses, underground trains and other forms of transport that everyone can use if they buy a ticket.

renewable energy – A natural source of energy that will not run out, such as wind power, solar power or wave power.

solar cells/solar panel – A device that can convert the power of the sun into electricity.

sound barrier – The increased drag and other forces that act on an object that is approaching the speed of sound.

sustainable – An action that avoids using up resources.

WEBSITES

www.bbc.com/future/tags/sustainability

Collection of BBC articles relating to sustainability and the future of science and technology.

http://science.howstuffworks.com/mega-machines-videos-playlist.htm

Videos explaining the work of various mega-machines.